Portable Guide to World Religions

A Quick Resource For At Home and Away

First Edition

Delton Krueger

A Religions Information Book

Morgen Krueger Ltd
Bloomington, Minnesota, USA

Morgen Krueger Ltd Publishing
PO Box 201804
Bloomington, Minnesota 55420 USA

Library of Congress Cataloging-in-Publication Data

Krueger, Delton
Portable Guide to World Religions: A Quick Resource for at Home and Away
Includes an index and bibliographic references.
ISBN-978-0-6151-3790-2

Cover design and printing by Lulu.com
First Edition

Contents

Chapter 2   Brief Summaries of Religions

Chapter 3   Comparisons of World Religions

Portable Guide to World Religions

FOREWORD

This book had its inception in the neighborhood of Mall of America in Minnesota during the 1990s. Representatives of several Christian churches gathered to deal with the impact of the nation's largest shopping and entertainment venue.

The Mall Area Religious Council developed as Jewish, Muslim, Baha'i, Hindu, Buddhist, and Unitarian representatives joined with a variety of Christians to create a spiritual presence.

It soon became evident that people of various religions could work together and relate with the public in a large commercial center.

It also became evident that contact between people of world religions was rather simple at first and then became more complicated as participants came to know more about each faith.

The international clientele of the Mall of America has brought the world to the American Midwest and has revealed that most people here know little about each religion and culture. Stereotypes are often simplistic and sometimes incorrect.

This realization triggered efforts to develop knowledge formats that can assist in the learning process and meet the desires of curious people – especially at places like major airports and shopping malls.

This book is a basic presentation of some elemental facts and opinions about world religions. Curious people are the audience.

Learning about religions appears to be a backward process. First one has stereotypes and vague impression. As time goes by more impressions come into view. At some point the curious person realizes that going into the elemental facts of life about religions seems like a backward process. One says, "Why did I not know or realize this earlier?" The basics help to fit the seemingly endless facts and impressions in a more understandable picture of religions – including ones own faith.

Future editions will reflect continuing learning in this field of growing relevance and importance – the religions of the world.

Delton Krueger

A Quick Resource for at Home and Away

Selected Data Points

of

World Religions

Chapter One

Selected Data Points

Several specific points of information enable a person to quickly begin the process of opening religions to personal view.

The Value of Data Points

- ***Origin*** -- Where on the earth did this religion have its start and at about what time in history – that is what origins are about. Some faiths arose in quite specific places and others began in the distant past with no records left for coming generations. The term "common era" or c.e. is used to relate with the Gregorian calendar for this study. Some religions claim to have been present from the beginning of the universe.

- ***Key Personality*** -- Most religions look to a figure, either historical or mythical, who gave teachings or life examples to which the religion looks for continuing definition. It could be said that the surest way to grasp the heart and soul of a religion is to learn about the founder or founders.

- *Primary Sacred Texts* -- Most religions have one or more written documents that are used to pass on the ideas and stories of the tradition. Their "sacredness" depends on the tradition. Some see them as the very words of the deity – others understand the text to be human expressions derived from the deity. Others treat the text as purely educational

  tools with minimal authority. Only one or two are noted in this survey. Links to further sources are provided in the Bibliography section. Oral tradition is used by some religions to transmit their meaning.

- *Numbers* -- The number of people determines the order for the listing of religions in this document – from the most to the least. The numbers are taken from the most reliable sources available today. A list of the sources is at the close of this section. In most instances the numbers are based on self reporting by religious organizations. Some religions have no organization. Here estimates are done by a variety of authorities in the fields of religion, business, and government. The total population count of the earth is presently about 6 billion 400 million people.

- *Trajectory* -- Where is this religion going? What appears to be the goal of efforts by the leaders and adherents? Naturally this is rather general statement. All belief systems have to do with meaning in life. Religions have as a primary function the giving of meaning. That is what trajectory is about – it is the direction toward which life moves, as understood in a particular religion.

- **Religions are listed in the following order:**

    Christianity

    Islam

    Hindu

    Chinese Traditional

    Buddhist

    Sikh

    Judaism

    Baha'i

    Shinto

    Jain

    Wicca / Neo Pagan

    Indigenous

    Materialist – Atheist – Secular

    Additional Belief Systems

Christianity

Place of origin	Present-day Israel and Palestine 50 c.e. (About 2000 years ago)
Key personality	Jesus Christ 4 b.c.e.-30 c.e.
Key words	Compassion – Justice – Resurrection
Sacred texts	Bible (Hebrew Scriptures and New Testament)
Numbers	About 2.1 billion people – 33% of world population
Trajectory	Justice and peace on earth, eternal life in God

Islam

Place of origin	Present-day Saudi Arabia
	622 c.e. (About 1400 years ago)
Key personality	Muhammad 560-632 c.e.
Key words	Submission to Allah – Mercy
Sacred texts	The Qur'an and The Hadith
Numbers	About 1.3 billion people – 19% of world population
Trajectory	World wide community of Islam, eternal life in Allah.

Hindu

Place of origin	India
	2000 b.c.e. (About 4000 years ago)
Key personality	Krishna
Key words	Santana Dharma (ancient religion) – Karma
Sacred texts	Rig Veda, Upanishad
Numbers	About 900 million people – 14% of world population
Trajectory	Soul finds release from the birth/death cycle

Chinese Traditional – Confucian and Daoist

Place of origin	China
	500 b.c.e. (About 2500 years ago)
Key personality	Confucius 551-479 b.c.e.
	Lao-Tzu 531-479 b.c.e.
Key words	Confucian – Duty, manners, wisdom
	Daoist – Yin and yang of life
Sacred texts	Writings of Confucius and Lao-Tzu
Numbers	About 394 million people – 6% of worl population
Trajectory	Harmonious national life and struggle of natural forces

Buddhist

Place of origin	India
	500 b.c.e. (About 2500 years ago)
Key personality	Siddhartha Gautama 566-486 b.c.e.
Key words	The Enlightened One (Buddha)
Sacred texts	Theravada and Mahayana scriptures
Numbers	About 376 million people – 5.8% of wo population
Trajectory	Individuals practice mindfulness and the Buddha nature

Sikh

Place of origin	India – Punjab province
	1500 c.e. (About 500 years ago)
Key personality	Guru Nanak 1469-1539 c.e.
Key words	Teaching, equality, service
Sacred texts	Guru Granth Sahib
Numbers	About 23 million people – .04% of wor population
Trajectory	The pure soul escapes rebirth and rests with creator

Judaism

Place of origin	Present-day Israel, Palestine, Arabia, and Egypt
	2000 b.c.e. (About 4000 years ago)
Key personality	Abraham 1200 b.c.e.
Key words	Covenant, the Ten Commandments
Sacred texts	The Torah (Hebrew Scriptures)
Numbers	About 14 million people – .022% of wo population
Trajectory	Movement toward justice, mercy, knowledge and identity

Baha'i

Place of origin	Iran
	1844 c.e. (About 160 years ago)
Key personality	Baha'u'llah (Siyyid Ali-Muhammad)
	1818-1892 c.e.
Key words	Unity of races, religions and nations
Sacred texts	Writings of Baha'u'llah and Abdul Bah
Numbers	About 7 million people – .001% of worl population
Trajectory	A coming world civilization

Shinto

Place of origin	Japan
	Unknown time of beginning
Key personality	None
Key words	Order, purity, kami (spirit in nature)
Sacred texts	Kojiki, Nihonshoki
Numbers	About 4 million people – .06% of worlc population
Trajectory	Harmony with nature and nation

Jain

Place of origin	India
	540 b.c.e. (About 2500 years ago)
Key personality	Lord Mahavira
Key words	Simplicity, austerity, nonviolence
Sacred texts	The Tatvarathasutra Umaswati
Numbers	About 4.2 million people – .06% of wor population
Trajectory	Overcome bodily senses to reach purity of soul

Wicca/Neo Pagan

Place of origin	Northern Europe
	Various ancient and modern times
Key personality	Various priests and goddesses
Key words	Goddess, magik, nature
Sacred texts	Wicca Rede
Numbers	About 1 million
Trajectory	A world in harmony with natural forces

Indigenous

Including Yoruba, Shamanism, Native American religion, Santeria, Vodun, Orisha, Candomble, Spiritism, other regional traditions.

Place of origin	Africa, Australia, North America, Asia, Europe
	Ancient times
Key personality	Tribal and other local holy persons
Key words	Spirits, harmony with nature
Artifacts	Hieroglyphics, oral traditions, petroglyphs
Numbers	About 400 million – 6% of world population
Trajectory	Harmony with spirits and the world

Materialist – Atheist – Secular

Place of origin	All countries of the world
Key personality	Richard Dawkins is a spokesperson for the atheist perspective today
Key words	Material world, realism
Texts	Books, newspapers, Internet
Numbers	About 1.1 billion people – 16% of world population
Trajectory	Toward a world without religions

Additional Belief Systems

Zoroastrian   Originating in Iran in about 1500 b.c.e. with Zoroaster and using The Gathas as sacred text, this religion of about 2.6 million people, now known an Parsii, aims toward victory over dark evil through justice and wisdom.

Cao Dai   Originating in 1926 in Vietman with Ngo Van Chieu, this religion of about 4 million adherents, draws on Buddhist, Confucian, and Christian traditions.

Unitarian Universalist   Originating in 1793 and 1825, the two traditions came together in 1961. Drawing on religions and philosophies from around the world, this tradition of about 800,000 adherents, holds to a belief system that values individual opinion and moves toward justice, equity and compassion.

Scientology   Originating in the 1950s in the USA with L. Ron Hubbard, this religion deals with abnormal behavior patters and recovery of positive human development.

Rastrafaria Originating in Jamaica in 1953 with the leadership of Marcus Garvey, this religion of about 600,000 adherents revere Haile Selassie I and look to ascendancy of the black race.

Not covered in this information section are: Theosophy, Tenrikyo, New Age, Eckankar, Juche and many other developing religions.

Sources for numbers of adherents:

World Almanac 2006

  http://worldalmanac.com

Adherents.com

  http://www.adherents.com

Religion and Ethics of BBC

  http://www.bbc.co.uk/religion/religions

ReligiousTolerance.org

  http://www.religioustolerance.org

A Quick Resource for at Home and Away

Brief Summaries of World Religions

Chapter Two
Brief Summaries of World Religions

The Religions as ordered by numbers based primarily on World Almanac 2006

The Value of Quick Summaries

Christianity

Islam

Hindu

Chinese Traditional

Buddhist

Sikh

Judaism

Baha'i

Shinto

Jain

Wicca – Neo Pagan

Indigenous

Materialist – Atheist – Secular

Additional Belief Systems

The Value of Quick Summaries

A portable guide to world religions necessitates brief summaries. A complete understanding of belief systems demands a lifetime of study, travel and personal adventure. The summaries launch a person into setting before the inquiring mind a limited sketch of salient factors that form the background for continuing exploration.

The guidelines for writing the summaries involved these procedures: 1. Developing an inclusive list; 2. Information gathering and sifting; 3. Writing statements that are brief, consistent, and fair. What follows is an expansion on these procedures.

- **Inclusive:** All major traditions are included. It is important to understand that religion in this book is defined as "belief systems". This explains why the Nonreligious – Atheist – Secular category is included in addition to the more commonly understood religious traditions. Separation of traditional religions from the wider and inclusive cultural scene is no longer possible in the light of instant communication that has taken the place of guarded borders between belief systems.

- **Informative:** A gathering and sifting of information is both simpler and more complex in the age of Google and other search devices. Access to sources is at hand with Internet connection. The challenge lies in the amount and accuracy of information that can be discovered. No one person, group or organization can possibly have all the details in mind for making summaries. There is no printed disclaimer in this book. It is assumed that all studies and books provide only partial information. Some readers may see what is written in this book as unfair or incomplete in presentation. It is the best we can do now.

- **Brief :** Approximately the same number of words are used for the summary of each religion and tradition. This means that religions included range from over 2 billion adherents at the one extreme to about 600,000 on the other hand. The order of appearance is based mostly on number of adherents because no other system seemed practical.

- **A Glossary** is provided to deal with words that may be unfamiliar. Internet search using Google or other services is helpful in getting at the variety of meanings that cluster around words and concepts. Religions tend to give unique meaning to the use of words in their systems of communication. In the writing of this book the word "religion" is given a meaning that contrasts with what can be called normal usage. Here the word "religion" means a thought system that gives meaning to life and is shared by a number of people.

Christianity

Jesus Christ as Lord of all life, source of justice and compassion is central to the Christian way. Christians believe that Jesus was the human face of the supreme deity. The Bible tells the story of how the deity enters into the lives of people to lead them to responsibility on earth and to an eternal reality (heaven). Translation into various cultures is the process for global presence. Congregations of believers gather for prayer, fellowship and learning. Daily life is when the faith, hope and love of the religion are expressed. Sunday is the usually observed day for public worship in churches and homes. Primary subdivisions of Christianity are Catholic, Orthodox, Protestant, Anglican, and Pentecostal.

Islam

Submission to Allah by all of the world's people is a central vision of Islam. Muslims believe that Prophet Muhammad received the words of the Qur'an directly from the deity. The Qur'an and the Hadith present a complete way of life for adherents. Islamization of cultures is the process for global presence. Observance of witness, daily prayers, almsgiving, fasting primarily during Ramadan and pilgrimage to Mecca are focal points for the individual Muslim. Religion and government are intimately related in Islam. Friday is the usual day for prayer services and sermons at the mosque. Primary subdivisions of Islam are Sunni, Shia, Sufi, and Wahhabi.

Hindu

Birth, marriage and death happening within a universe of balance and ancient truth are central visions of the Hindu way. Diversity is known in the many traditions gathered under the umbrella of Hinduism. Karma governs the balance of life and underlies the belief in reincarnation. A variety of deities and gods/goddesses relate a supreme being to the daily experiences of life. Temples of all sizes across India and the world are the scene for offerings, prayers and teachings on all days of the week. Festivals mark the stages of life and provide for community celebrations. Vedic wisdom is valued. Rivers and trees have sacred meaning. There are a multitude of sects who venerate selected gods and goddesses.

Chinese Traditional

Confucian

Benevolence, duty, manners, wisdom and faithfulness are cardinal virtues for this major religious tradition of China. It is a secular religion in that there are no higher powers or deities. The creation of a society based on virtue and the practices of people in daily life are central. People are to behave appropriate to their position in life. Primary relationships are between parents and children, especially fathers and sons. Taoism and Buddhism share the religious scene in China with Confucianism.

Taoist

Attention to the cycles of nature and the way things return to their starting points distinguish the approach of this religion. The believer looks to tune in to the endless yin and yang of change through meditation and contemplation. All of life is made possible by ch'i, the breath of the universe. Childbirth, wealth and health are manifestations of the Tao. Temples have been rebuilt. The art of feng shui aims to help human constructions to be in harmony with the force that shape land and life.

Buddhist

Enlightenment involving understanding of suffering and the achievement of freedom in nirvana are central visions of the Buddhist tradition. Through the Four Noble Truths and Eightfold Path taught by Buddha the cycle of rebirth can be broken. His enlightenment revealed that desire is at the root of suffering and problems. Constant change and elimination of selfish desires are valued principles. There is no being, only becoming. Shrines, temples and monasteries are for meditation, discussion and retreat on all days of the week. Devotion to a buddha or bodhisattva as well as pilgrimages are encouraged. Festivals involve temple visits, alms-giving and offerings at shrines. Primary sub groups are Theravada, Mahayana, and Zen.

Sikh

Service, equality among people, and devotion to God in daily life are distinguishing characteristics of the Sikh people. Early development was in a Hindu and Muslim context. Guru Nanak was the first of some ten recognized teachers who represent the unknowable God - the Great Teacher. Gudwaras are places for prayer, music and the sharing of food on all days of the week. The defense of religious freedom led to formation of a brotherhood primarily for men - the Kalsa. The turban worn by men is a unique Sikh practice.

Judaism

Hope for the redemption of the world is a central vision of Judaism. Abraham entered into a covenant (agreement) with the one supreme deity. The Torah (first five books of the Hebrew Scriptures) gives an account of the people of Israel as they responded to the call of the deity toward peace and justice. The family is a focal point of religious observance, education and individual identity. A minority in most instances, Judaism highly values its ethnic identity. The sacred time of Sabbath begins on Friday sundown and continues to Saturday sundown. Worship is observed at the synagogue and in family events. Primary subdivisions of Judaism are Orthodox, Conservative, Reform, and Reconstructionist

Baha'i

The creation of one world of religion and government with justice for all is a central vision of Baha'i. Equality of men and women is valued. A belief in new revelations means that Baha'i sees itself as in a long line of religious traditions. Worship is to be daily; is primarily an individual decision; and involves three obligatory prayers. Fellowship occasions take place in homes. There are also centers for collective group prayers. Baha'i, a smaller religion in terms of constituent numbers, has gathered influence in many circles.

Shinto

A concern for continuity, balance and purity in life from early time in the families of historic Japan led to this present day religion. There was a period of state religion. Local, nature based religious observances are the present day expression. Shrines with special gateways exalt natural beauty and are focal points of worship as are home altars. Japanese Gardens in many countries exhibit the grace and harmony of this religion and its respect for the spirits (kami) present in natural world elements.

Jain

Contemplation is a central feature of the Jain life. Nonviolence and the ascetic life follow from the Jain conviction that all life is sacred and that cruelty to any creature degrades the universe - an uncreated and eternal reality. Everything has a soul. A primary goal is to break free from the cycle of rebirths. Passions and bodily senses are to be conquered by purity and perfection of the soul. This religion of India has a worldwide presence primarily carried by business persons.

Wicca - Neo Pagan

Primarily nature based, these traditions present spontaneous varieties of practices and philosophies, and have various formats across the world with concentration in northern Europe and North America. Organization is not a feature of their structures. Small community and kinship based life structure characterizes their presence. Some argue that Wicca and Neo Pagan systems are quite different. The opinion expressed here is that in the basic perspective they have enough in common to be grouped together

Indigenous

Examples are Native American religions of North America; Yoruba, Candomblé, Vodou and Santeria developed in Africa and also South America. The religions are based on oral traditions. Animal sacrifice, various Spirit influences, and supernatural events are characteristics of some. Australian Aboriginal religions for the most part consider their traditions as sacred and private. Native American religion practices are not for public viewing.

Materialist – Atheist – Secular

Persons in this realm are mostly passive in regard to traditional religions. Some are adherents of philosophies such as secular humanism, agnosticism, atheism, pantheism, and free thought. Some are aggressively opposed to religion. Most are simply non religious. Serious atheists actively promote the non existence of God and the abolition of traditional religions. Agnostics see God as incoherent and irrelevant to real life. Secular believers wish to be free from religious ideas based on superstition.

Additional Belief Systems

Zoroastrian - A promise of justice, immortality and bliss distinguish the early forms of this religion. The prophet Zoroaster (Zarathustra) presented ideas that appear in Judaism, Christianity, Islam and other major religions. Small Zoroastrian communities exist today in India and Iran and are known as Parsii.

Cao Dai - As a combination of a number of traditions primarily in Vietnam this religion takes ethics from Confucianism, Karma and rebirth from Buddhism and organization from the Roman Catholic Christian tradition.

Unitarian Universalist – Coming from Christian and Jewish roots, this tradition holds that personal experience, conscience and reason are the final authorities in matters of belief. Wisdom in approaching social and justice issues is a valued objective in life.

Scientology – This tradition is based on a form of psychotherapy originated by L. Ron Hubbard in the USA. Destructive imprints from previous experiences need to be dealt with in order for humans to be liberated.

Rastafaria – As a combination of African and Western thought this religion, with its beginnings in Jamaica, sees the black race as destined for greatness in the global future.

Other Traditions – See the Internet for further beliefs information on **Theosophy**, **Tenrikyo**, **New Age**, **Eckankar**, **Juche** and many more.

A Quick Resource for at Home and Away

Comparisons
of
World
Religions

Chapter Three

Comparisons between Religions
in order of appearance:

The Value of Comparisons

Sacred Texts

Sacred Places

Gender Issues

Foods and Dietary Practices

Music, Art and Culture

Religion and Government

Time and Observances

Cultural and Religious Taboos

The Value of Comparisons

A portable guide sets before the reader certain categories of experience shared by all traditions. Out of all the possible options a certain few are chosen, in this instance eight items.

Religions are encrusted with cultural practices and assumptions. Each faith system developed in a certain part of the global human community and carries the implanted nature of that region. Over time most religions have grown beyond isolated places and some have become truly global in nature. However the "cultural genetic tags" remain.

Geography shapes viewpoints. Desert people, mountain people, sea coast people and plains people experience life in unique ways. Religions carry the flavor of the lay of the land in which development has occurred. Geographic settings continue to influence the concepts, ideas, and practices of the faith systems.

Sacred and holy are words pointing to places, items, and events with special meaning for adherents of religions. Travelers and students soon learn that awareness of sacred places influences ones acceptance in a country or among a group. To be unaware of the sacred is to offend the host people. Access to human interchange and friendship depends to a great degree on the visitor's appreciation for that which is understood to be holy. Comparison of various traditions trains the mind to pay attention to new realities in new places. Effective first impressions of religions depend on having some basic knowledge of a tradition.

Sacred Texts

Religions hold their chosen documents as sacred or instructive. Some see the documents as valued historical information. Others see them as the very words of the divine source of their faith. Some use them as wisdom for living life now. Some include words of the founders and others present reflections by disciples, gurus, or authority figures. Poetry and prose are sometimes used. Pictures or icons are valued by some and dismissed by others.

One can avoid misunderstandings and unintentional offense by being aware of the role taken by the texts, sacred or secular. Avoid handling the books, scrolls or other text formats in a disrespectful manner. Show interest in the attitude of the individuals with whom one is speaking toward their sacred texts, pictures, objects and places. For some, the "text" is a place in the natural world.

Christianity: The *Bible*, made up of the Hebrew Scriptures (Old Testament) and the New Testament is the central scripture for believers. Orthodox and Catholic traditions accept the *Apocrypha* as well as traditional scripture. Some Christians accept the Bible as literal in its accounts and supreme in its authority. Other believers receive the Bible as a spiritually inspired statement of the faith in a particular time and place which needs translation and interpretation for each era time. Yet others see the Bible as a book of wisdom and guidance for daily life. The Bible is always translated into the languages of the people of a place. Analytic study of the Bible is generally encouraged.

Islam: The *Qur'an* is understood to be the very words of Allah (God) revealed to the Prophet Muhammad. Arabic is the language of the Qur'an and is universally used in Islamic devotion and study. Additional words of Muhammad and learned scholars, The *Sunna* and the *Hadith,* are remembrances of Muhammad and interpretations of the *Qur'an* for the guidance of an entire way of life. Words of the Qur'an are to be learned and said aloud often. Believers are expected to learn Arabic and say the words of the Qur'an in Arabic. The use of transliteration is used when Arabic is not known. Analytic study of the *Qur'an* has not been encouraged but new approaches are being considered.

Hindu: *The Bhagavad Gita* is the most widely used text. The *Vedas* are the most ancient texts with the *Rig Veda* as the oldest and of special importance. The *Upanishads* are primarily a collection of doctrinal writings. The Law Codes offer societal regulations and the *Puranas* are of historical interest. *The Ramayana* is an epic folk story used widely in the culture of India. Ritual and philosophy books are many and widely valued. Texts serve as devotional expressions and cultural resources.

Buddhist: Various sects recognize different texts that draw on the same basic traditions. *The Tripitaka* (Sanskrit) and *Tipitaka* (Pali) are the foundation documents for all Buddhist teachings. For centuries the tradition was transmitted orally and in the first century b.c.e. a written record first appears. The wide array of original documents and translations means there is no one collection of Buddhist scriptures. The sutras are a widely used record of the teachings and conversations of the Buddha. Writings of sages and scholars are additional scriptures. Texts include doctrinal, philosophical and interpretive literature.

Chinese Religions - Confucian/Daoist/Buddhist:

The many writings by followers of Confucius feature the *Six Classics* and the *Four Books*. The *Analects* are most well known. The primary focus is on social order. In the Daoist tradition the *Tao Te Ching* related with Lao Tzu and the *Zhuangzi* focus on the importance of pattern and order in the here and now. There are thousands of written works focused on stories of nature and people. The Buddhist tradition has the *Lotus Sutra* and *Songs of the South* as important writings.

Sikh: The *Guru Granth Sahib*, the primary sacred text is composed of a collection of hymns and wisdom used in public events. Secondary texts are *Dasam Granth* and *Nit nem*. They are used for private devotion. Reading from the sacred texts is understood as service to God. The texts themselves are primary teachers for the faithful. At Gudwaras (Temples) the *Guru Granth Sahib* is displayed on a Palki – a special platform.

Judaism: *The Torah* is the central Hebrew Scripture. The Hebrew Bible, composed of 24 books, is the basic source for all teachings. Those scriptures are understood to be sacred in the sense of being here as a guide for life, for study and for interpretation. The *Mishnah* and *Talmud* are a collections of Rabbinic teachings. The sacred scrolls, hand written, are focal points in the synagogue.

Bahá'i: The writings of Bahá'u'llah are spoken of as *The Tablets*. The *Kitáb-i-Aqdas* contain laws to govern Baha'i society, establish holidays, and set moral principals. Revelations to Baha'u'lláh, The Báb and 'Abdu'l-Bahá are texts accepted as superceding the scriptures of other religions.

Shinto: Stories and mythic tales are gathered in the *Kojiki* (Record of ancient events), *Nihongi* (Chronicles of Japan) and *Engishiki* (Ritual and ceremonial instructions). *Judoki* are provincial chronicles. There are also mythic tales of Amaterasu and her descendents as well as origin of the kami (spirits). Buddhist writings such as the *Lotus Sutra* are influential.

Jain: The two main sects have different texts. Both recognize the twelve books called *Angas*. The Svetambara sect uses the *Kalpa Sutra* at festivals. The Digambara sect uses works by Kundakemda and the *Siddhanta* texts. The messages of founder Lord Mahavira are found in Buddhist texts.

Wicca – Neo Pagan: Collections of ancient myths and ceremonial guidelines are widely used. Wicca uses *The Book of Shadows* in particular. Individual adherents create their own personal texts. Present day experience rather than authoritative texts or leaders mark this tradition.

Indigenous Religions: Petroglyphs and other forms of rock drawings are the form of Sacred Texts of some of the tribes and ancient religious societies. The spoken word and oral traditions are the primary method for passing on the myths and stories that give meaning for life today. Natural objects and sites as well as ceremonial dances and rituals are among the ways of communicating the stories of the tradition.

Materialist – Atheist – Secular: The texts of this perspective are the books, journals, addresses and other documents which have arisen over the ages and that display the investigations and thoughts of people. Scientific and academic studies producing new knowledge are highly valued. Commercial and business models and practices are highly documented in newspapers, journals, books, and on the Internet. Electronic communication media are dominated by this perspective. There is no central body of documents that prevail.

Sacred Places

All religions have designated places representing either the origin of the faith, or a great event for adherents of that faith. Each site takes on spiritual meaning and becomes an emotional center for the faith. Some sites are shared by several traditions, the most well known being Jerusalem shared by Jew, Christian and Muslim

Pilgrimages to sacred sites draw great numbers to various regions of the earth. People involved on pilgrimage are magnets for commercial ventures which supply necessities for the people and also offer remembrances that can be purchased.

For some religions it is offensive for visitors to take pictures at sacred sites. Treating the entire place with reverence is appropriate behavior. Speak with adherents to learn appropriate behavior at the sacred site.

Christianity: Historic events in Jerusalem and the surrounding country side are the early history of this faith. Rome and Constantinople have long standing importance in the history of Catholic and Orthodox traditions. Pilgrimages are often made to sites of healings and appearances of holy figures. All Christian traditions have churches, cathedrals and sacred sites in all regions of the world.

Islam: Mecca and Medina immediately come to mind. The Hajj is a pilgrimage to this holy center expected at least one time by all able bodied Muslims who can travel there and take part in the annual rituals. Jerusalem is also the location for historic Islamic sites. Other sites include mosques commemorating persons and events important in the history of Islam as well as geographic locations with historic meaning.

Hindu: Rivers of India are sacred sites for pilgrimages and for ashes of the dead. Temples and shrines are where people gather to make offerings, pray, sing, and listen to teaching. Village temples, presided over by priests, are usually dedicated to Shiva and Vishnu. Home shrines with images of gods and goddesses are frequent. Trees and mountains are respected for spiritual powers.

Buddhist: Temples accompanied by pagodas and stupas are wide spread in India and in China. Statues and paintings adorn shrines in homes and temples. Pilgrimages to places that are important in the life of Buddha are valued. The Bodhi tree in Northern India is of special interest as the traditional site of Gautama Buddha's achievement of Nirvana.

Chinese Religions - Confucian/Daoist/Buddhist: The landscape of China is seen as reflecting the yin and yang of the natural order. Feng shui design intends to create buildings and décor that is in harmony with nature. Daoist temples in cities are tended by monks and nuns. There are also Buddhist and Confucian temples. Mountains and other natural phenomena are seen as having spiritual power.

Sikh: Temples (Gudwaras) are places for worship and always have a kitchen and dining for the weekly presentation of food for all who come. Some elaborate Sikh temples are in the Punjab region of India.

Judaism: Jerusalem and its region are unquestionably central to the Jewish tradition. For Judaism the entire early history of the faith was centered on this location for the early temple for worship and education. It continues to be an emotional and spiritual center for adherents. Temples and synagogues are central gathering points for the Jewish community which is distributed all across the earth.

Baha'i: Haifa, Israel is the location of the prime governing body – The Universal House of Justice. Shrines honoring the founders are also at Haifa. Temples in various world cities are centers of collective prayer for people of all faiths.

Shinto: Shrines are places for worship and community gathering. A torii archway gate is always at the entry to a temple. Shrines range from very small to large constructions. The landscape is designed to express harmony between the human and natural worlds. Home altars are often present in villages and cities.

Jain: The temple on Mount Abu and the statue of Bahubali in Karnataka are the most well known centers of Jain pilgrimage in India today. Temples are being built in a variety of cities. The Jain life of asceticism and nonviolence does not lend itself to wealth and buildings.

Wicca - Neo Pagan: Wicca, Druid and other sub groups have centers mostly in the United Kingdom, the United States and in Scandinavia. Standing Stone sites are often centers of attention. Sites in nature, seen as full of divine life, are used for rituals and holy days

Indigenous: Sacred sites are of unique importance to the various religions that have tribal and regional identities. They are scattered across all inhabited continents and are often known only to tribal and kinship groups. The various elements of nature have sacred meaning.

Materialist – Atheist – Secular: Sites of importance are either a personal choice, a national site of importance, or business monuments. All of these sites depend on regional and national cultural life. Persons with environmental concerns and a respect for the earth place high value on undisturbed natural regions. The wider universe is also of interest as a place where other beings may exist. Scientific study of all things may have a purely utilitarian or commercial value or may be understood by some as verging on the sacred.

Gender Issues

Any form of contact between female and male, male and male, female and female, raise important identity issues in all world religions. Cultures and religions understand gender issues to be of elementary importance.

Respect for the traditions of the community and culture in which one finds oneself is basic. One may well be quite surprised at the rules, unspoken and spoken, that apply. Gender issues are highly personal and deeply ingrained. To offend the host culture or religion in these matters can be life threatening in some regions.

- *The body of a person is private space – not to be violated.*

- *Looking at a person is always meaning filled – caution is advised.*

- *Show personal respect at all times and in all places. Gender regulations and taboos are difficult to describe, remember or manage. Here are some basic understandings that prevail in the world's great religions.*

Christianity: The dignity of all persons, male and female, is a central principle of this faith. Cultural practices regarding authority of men and women vary widely, depending on the country and region. Women are taking increasing leadership roles in many traditions. Some Christian bodies do not allow women to take leadership roles. Family life is always the basic Christian community. Gender issues are open to discussion.

Islam: Clear and definite roles for men and women are central to the practices of this religion. For women, modesty and covering the body in public are necessities. Men are to be protectors of women. Men have a public role in prayers and community life. Privacy of family life is the accepted pattern. It is offensive in some Muslim cultures for a non-Muslim to touch or directly approach a Muslim woman. Traditional gender roles are usually not open to discussion.

Hindu: Men and women have traditional roles that are presently being examined and in some instances changing. Education for women is on the increase. Property inheritance rights for women are increasing. Men receive primary attention in many aspects of social life. Marriage and having children is an honored calling in life. Gender issues are becoming open for discussion.

Buddhist: Although leadership and teaching has been primarily a male function, women are taking a more active role in Buddhist culture. Some schools of thought believe that women cannot attain full enlightenment. The feminine side of compassion is respected. Monastic life is highly valued and involves men and women as monks and nuns. Gender issues are open for discussion.

Chinese Religions - **Confucian/Daoist/Buddhist**: Traditional religion appears to support a patriarchal society in China. Government efforts to institute legal gender equality are presently being tested by "market socialism" and its market driven forces. Preference for males is evident particularly in the countryside. Gender issues are fluid and changing.

Sikh: Men have primary leadership roles and women are seen as bearers of the religion in the home. The public role of women tends to be restricted, especially in India. The Khalsa, a brotherhood to fight oppression and for justice, is primarily men, however, women may join the Khalsa. Gender issues are open for discussion.

Judaism: Equality of men and women, each with specific roles, is central to the tradition. Males are traditional spiritual leaders. Women are increasingly taking this role as well. Females tend to manage the home with its food practices and child rearing. It is expected that men and women will marry and raise children. Gender roles are discussed.

Baha'i: Equality of men and women as well as balance between masculine and feminine qualities, are priorities for society. The founder's vision for a new world is one "permeated with feminine ideas." Leadership on most levels is shared between men and women. Gender issues are open for discussion.

Shinto: In Japan the family is the main preserver of tradition and women take much of the responsibility. It is reported that men do little housework, rearing of children or caring for the elderly. Violence against women is a continuing concern. The religious traditions of Shinto and Buddhism teach that all human life is sacred but there is not a clear moral code. Gender equality is being strongly encouraged by the government with new laws passed in 1999 and 2000. Women are moving into more leadership roles in business and government.

Jain: Considering the ascetic goal of fighting against passion and bodily senses in order to reach purity of soul, most gender related issues would be distractions. The austere life of a monk involves avoids injuring any life form and, among other practices, will not have sexual intercourse. Women appear to have a minor role in this religion.

Wicca – Neo Pagan: The strong role of feminism in these religious traditions presents sexuality as a positive spiritual influence. Goddesses are honored as part of the annual cycle of death and rebirth in mythical stories. Male gods are also part of mythology. Equality of the sexes is promoted.

Indigenous Religions: Males and females share in sacred and other leadership roles depending on the particular tradition. The role of males and females in society differs widely between various tribal groups. Powers of reproduction are often seen as evidence of the sacred.

Materialist – Atheist – Secular: Gender is involved in all aspects of social life. Since religious guidelines are not applicable, prudent decision making is based on the dominant values of the region. Sex is often used for commercial purposes in terms of advertising, in the pornography business, and throughout the entertainment industry. There is no recognizable moral framework within which gender issues may be understood. A pragmatic outlook on gender realities applies to the role of family life; health care; the criminal justice system, social welfare, and educational practices. Gender issues are open to discussion.

Foods and Dietary Practices

Food is more than nourishment for the body in religious traditions. Long held beliefs and practices may represent health concerns and family gathering rites. The rituals of food preparation and eating/drinking are unique to each culture and religion. Food practices are one way to maintain group identity in a global environment. People are usually quite eager to inform the visitor about their foods. Local practices are to be observed and honored by visitors.

Sharing of food is a sign of hospitality in most religious traditions. Welcome for the stranger and visitor is often in a mealtime or feast venue. Sacred times are often observed with food sharing at Feast Days. Fasting from food at certain times is a central part of some traditions.

In some religions the most sacred of rituals use food as symbols of their sacred beliefs and traditions. Respect for dietary practices that may at first glance seem bizarre is important for developing respectful relationships. Adherents of religions are usually quite eager to explain the meaning of their practices.

Christianity: There are no universally prohibited foods. National and local Christian groups may emphasize certain practices such as vegetarian diet and regular fasting schedules. Healthy diet practices are part of the faith system for some Christian groups. Sharing of food in church gatherings is a basic element of Christianity. All world cultural practices regarding foods are reflected in regional Christian attitudes regarding foods. If alcohol is acceptable, temperate usage is expected.

Islam: "Halal" foods are those prepared with accepted Muslim practices. "Haram" are forbidden foods including all pork and related items as well as all alcohol related items. The place of food in showing hospitality to visitors and strangers is valued in Islam. Both feasting and fasting are observed. Many national food practices have been influenced by Muslim/Arabic styles of food production and consumption. The month of Ramadan, given to fasting during day light hours, is a central part of religious observance.

Hindu: The food practices of India are reflected in most Hindu communities. There are no strictly observed food practices. Emphasis on a vegetarian diet as well as use of unique spices, especially curries, is observed. The enjoyment of foods that are consistent with physical and spiritual health is encouraged. Some groups prohibit the eating of beef and pork products as well as poultry, fish and eggs. Food is important to worship. Fast days are also widely observed.

Buddhist: A vegetarian diet accompanied by moderation and some fasting is encouraged in all Buddhist groups. The principle of ahimsa referring to non-violent treatment of animals informs dietary practices. Belief in karma relates to food, eating and taste as illusions. Enlightenment is preferred to personal satisfaction. No clear distinction is made between permitted and forbidden foods.

Chinese Religions - Confucian/Daoist/Buddhist

Chinese dietary practices are observed. Confucius taught that "food is the force binding society together." Vegetables, rice and relatively less meat is typical. The yin and yang balance is applied to food and diet. Tea is a main drink in the country. Banquets are often at times of celebration and are a token of welcome.

Sikh: Eating together affirms human equality. Alcohol, tobacco and non-medicinal drugs are not to be used. Halal and Kosher meats that involve ritual slaughter are not to be eaten. Some adherents eat no beef or pork. A vegetarian diet is preferred. Providing meals for visitors to the Gudwara (place of worship) is widely practiced.

Judaism: Strict regulations about food production, preparation and consuming are universal in Jewish practice. The term "kosher" indicates obedience to accepted production regulations. Traditions vary on the detail of regulations and the consistency of application. Certain foods such as pork and shell fish are universally prohibited. Traditional recipes and methods for preparation are important elements of Jewish identity. Alcohol usage is sometimes part of important religious observances.

Baha'i: There are no dietary restrictions. Alcohol and recreational drugs are forbidden. Dietary customs of the country of residence prevail.

Shinto: Japanese dietary practices are observed. A variety of foods are to be eaten. Mealtime is to be pleasurable. Home cooking is encouraged. Tea is widely used. People are encouraged to eat so as to manage body weight and health.

Jain: Among vows for lay persons are the avoidance of meat, wine, honey, fruits, roots and night eating. Monks have more stringent dietary regulations. For some, avoidance of food leading to starvation is a virtuous life story. Austerity marks this faith.

Wicca Neo Pagan: There are no commonly accepted dietary regulations. Many adherents are vegetarian.

Indigenous: Every regional and kinship group has its own food and dietary regulations and expectations. Practices usually depend on the available plants and animals of the region and success in obtaining the food.

Materialist, atheist, secular: There are no agreed upon food practices that prevail in this sector of the human family. Safety in preparation of foods is expected. Healthy foods are often highly valued for the sake of personal health and a productive life. Alcohol and related substances are frequently used.

Music, Art and Culture

Each religion has unique practices and opinions regarding artistic expression. The appearance of public spaces often reflects a religious tradition. Certain taboos are most clearly observed in artistic expressions. Attitudes toward the body, colors, and shapes grow out of the sense of meaning developed in any particular tradition.

Tourism often capitalizes on these unique expressions in appealing to visitors interested in the new and unusual. Exploration of sites and scenes beyond the tourist circuit offer an even broader exposure to the religion and culture. Religion and custom are often so intertwined that one can hardly tell one from the other. This is an endless field of travel, exploration and surprises.

Christianity: Music is a central feature in Christian worship and cultural expression. The combination of sacred words with sounds is unique in all of the national regions where this religion has a place. Christianity brings, not a culture, but an idea about faith, to each place. The faith is translated into the dominant languages and art forms. Jesus and his Holy Mother Mary are universal features of Christian art forms. The human body is accepted as an appropriate format for artistic expression. Some forms of Christianity wish to avoid overly great attention to human creations and are simple and austere in cultural expression. Most Christian worship features liturgical forms, a calendar of festival days, singing of hymns, psalms and songs. There is no one accepted artistic expression within Christianity.

Islam: The power of unique sounds and of artistic expressions that use geometric design rather than human or animal forms gives a special flavor to art wherever Islam is present. The words of *Qur'an* in Arabic are sacred to Muslims whether spoken or written in artistic formats. Creative expressions that attempt to give form to Allah are not acceptable. The human body is not to be exalted in artistic expressions. Sounds growing out of Arab culture appear wherever Islam has significant presence. Covering the body is important, especially for females. Islam brings its culture to each and every location in its global expression. Musical chants, calls to prayer, art and culture are primary factors in extension of the Muslim religion.

Hindu: Festivals and pilgrimages provide occasions for dance and music. Some say that Brahman - the supreme being - is present in sound itself. Color, lights, decoration, new clothing, fireworks, tinted water – all are part of various festivals in honor of deities. Dance and music are seen as routes to religious experience. Drama is often a way of telling the stories of the gods. Sacred dance elements were first spelled out in *The Natya Shastra* (200 b.c.e.). Hindu shaped culture is enlivened by the many celebrations and festivals. Hinduism is a term describing all the cultures of India and is inclusive of the multitude of religions that exist in the country.

Buddhist: The Awakening of Buddha and his teachings are focal points in much art and culture of the Buddhist way. There are grand monuments to The Wheel of Dharma and the Bodhi Tree. Sculptures of Buddha are aids to meditation. The Mandala (Sacred Circle) representing the individual believer and the universe is used in many artistic creations. Wall painting and temples themselves are display of the teachings about finding serenity in a world of suffering and change. Koan, a form of riddle, is a way of showing the limits of human knowledge. Tranquil gardens, flower arranging, and tea ceremonies are integrated into meditative practice.

Sikh: The teachings of scripture are set to music and used at worship at temples (Gudwaras). Artistic style is seen in the décor of places of worship. As the center of activity for the Sikh community, the Gudwara features display rooms for the Scriptures, prayers, and food distribution.

Judaism: The portable arts - music, literature, painting and performance - are clearly distinctive in the Jewish tradition. Coming from a history of having buildings and sites destroyed over and again, the Jewish community focuses on the family and individual creative expression. Argument and debate rise to a performance level of skill. Dramatic and musical performances entertain and express the vital life of a people disbursed across world. To excel in artistic expression is held as a high priority in Judaism. Synagogues express in architecture the high value placed on scrolls of The Torah and community of believers.

Baha'i: Music, pictures and poetry are expressions of the vision for a world of unity and peace in Baha'i. The Shrine of the Bab and the Baha'i World Center administrative buildings in Haifa feature gardens and other artistic displays. Believers are encouraged to excel in artistic creation in whatever country and culture they may be found. Celebrations with dance and sharing of food mark Baha'i community life.

Shinto: Shrines offer people a place for worship and to find serenity. Located in a grove of trees and approached over a pond spanned by a sacred bridge and a gate called a Torii, the shrine exhibits the respect shown to spirits of nature. Home shrines are also an expression of creative respect. Japanese music and art are the common expression of the Shinto outlook.

Chinese   Religions-Confucian/Daoist/Buddhist:

The ancient art of Feng shui represents a strong desire to restore balance to the yin and yang of the landscape. Buildings and natural features need to be in harmony as does the internal arrangement of buildings. Artistic rendition of the Buddha and Confucius adorn temples and shrines. Painting, exercise, yoga, cooking and medicine are ways of showing harmony and balance.

Jain: In the light of a principal of detachment from material things there is little concern for buildings or artistic developments. Material pleasures are seen as transitory illusions and distractions from meditation and promoting humanitarian causes. Temples are dedicated to worship and various ceremonies.

Wicca – Neo Pagan: Emphasis on the changing of the seasons mean that rituals and artistic creations focus on nature in its variety. Goddess worship is expressed in music and artistic creations. An emphasis on the feminine is a prominent feature of the culture of this tradition.

Indigenous: Technology is not a part of the life of persons in these religious expressions. Artistic expressions often exhibit highly skilled people at work and at play. Culture is a here and now experience with little commercial impact or concern for public exhibition.

Materialist – Atheist – Secular: The power of secular culture to create music, dance, and art is amazing. Use of contemporary technology means that new forms are persistently arising. Those forms are then replaced by the next new expression and so it continues. At times it is difficult to tell the difference between religious and secular artistic expression.

A Quick Resource for at Home and Away

Religion and Government

As a universal presence, religions interface with every form of civil government that has existed and does now exist. Relationships range from religion and government being one and the same, to a complete separation of religion and secular government. As history moves along, religions change in their relationship with the governing authorities. Political issues related to this matter are debated far and wide. In the 21st century this subject appears to be growing in importance with implications for world peace, ecological survival, and human development.

Historical events such as councils when critical decisions were made, battles when people of a particular religion prevailed, birthdays, deaths and martyrdoms of religious figures are all ways of giving power to religious traditions as they maintain their identities in the context of changing governments. The governments may be tribal leaders, powerful dictatorial forces, elected legislative formats, or less formal entities that maintain some form of community life.

Christianity: Existing in the midst of all forms of government Christians have in some places been a dominating influence and in others a tolerated or persecuted minority. The Catholic tradition inherited from the Roman Empire certain forms of organization and national ambition. Protestant movements challenged this situation and, for the most part, separated religion from the secular state. Christians see the religious community as beyond and above all nations and governments. Primary allegiance of Christian people is to God. This is a serious problem for some nations when powerful leaders/groups punish what they deem to be disloyalty. .

Islam: In the ideal world of Islam religion and government are one and the same. A goal of Islam is a world community obedient to Muslim law and cultural norms. Beginning with the struggle of Muhammad to make place for a religion of one God in the Arab world, the history of Islam is one of struggle (jihad). Islam looks to a restoration of the glory and strength experienced during some historical periods. Conflict between Muslim minorities in countries with secular governments is a growing source of tension. Allegiance to Allah is the primary loyalty for all Muslims.

Hindu: As an umbrella for a large number of sects and groups, Hinduism focuses on the family and community as providers of rituals that hold life together. In India, the homeland of Hinduism, a secular government aims to practice religious tolerance. All religions have equal status before the law. There is no real boundary between sacred and secular in the Hindu approach to religion. Political parties in India often reflect the outlook of the primary constituents and their religious tradition.

Buddhist: Throughout its history, Buddhism has at times been the teacher in a society and at other times has been intertwined with government in shaping the culture, even to the point of being a state religion in some regions Accommodation is the pattern in most countries and cultures. Viewing itself as a way of life for all cultures, Buddhist adherents take the ways of a particular nation and shape their personal lives for loyalty to basic Buddhist principles while integrating with the national culture.

Chinese Religions - Confucian/Daoist/Buddhist: An overall concern to live harmoniously within family, society and nature in the context of a well ordered society with each person playing their proper role is central to Chinese culture. The constant changes of the universe and the everlasting struggle between good and bad are an assumed reality. To exist within the given framework of life is a guiding principle. At one time, religion was of central influence in governmental matters. Having lived through an era of religious oppression, adherents of Chinese religions are today a focus for many families and individual persons.

Sikh: As a minority with a dominant influence in the Punjab state of India, Sikhism has had significant influence on governmental practices. With a strong belief in the power and justice of God, believers intend to influence social practice wherever they live. A commitment to hard work and liberation of the individual has led to active participation in many world societies.

Judaism: As a historic minority wherever Jewish people have lived, Jews have learned how to manage life by developing their strengths and being persistent. Some governments have brought tragic persecution on Jews and others have actively protected their minority status. Jewish people are active in governments of many countries. The place of the nation of Israel in the community of nations is complicated by relationships with the Arab world involving long term antagonisms.

Baha'i: The vision of one world government encourages a persistent effort by adherents to move toward peaceful world unity. In some countries Baha'i adherents have experienced violent persecution. Through local units that take active role in their communities this religion sees itself as a patient and persistent world influence.

Shinto: At one time the state religion of Japan, Shinto practice now is focused on harmony and order which is welcomed as a stabilizing influence in society. Today the Imperial family continues to honor personal traditional rituals. Almost entirely contained in Japan, Shinto with its focus on nature and worship in serene surroundings is of interest to a growing wider global audience. Coupled in many ways with Buddhism, Shinto philosophy provides rituals as well as ties with past generations.

Jain: A strong tradition of simplicity and rejection of materialism means that believers have little interest in national adventures and policies.

Wicca – Neo Pagan: As nature based religions with individual and small group identities, this tradition has little or no interest in relating with the government other than concern over legal identity, access problems, and environmental issues.

Indigenous religions: The tribal nature of certain groups, such as Native Americans, means that issues of national sovereignty are of significant importance. In Africa and South America the preservation of indigenous tribes and culture raise issues of national controls over commercial invasions of tribal lands and peoples. Tribal groups may be part of anti governmental movements in some regions. The religions bring passion to these recognition efforts.

Materialist – Atheist – Secular: These traditions are often the central reality of government. Only in theocratic states would the secular presence be discouraged. At times government is used to control religions and to sideline them. In other times and places accommodation between religions and government provide mutual benefit. At other times governments have set out to destroy all people of certain religions. This is a volatile and evolving field of thought and practice.

Time and Observances

The rhythm of time reflects the soul of a culture and a religion. Religious traditions were the first to establish orderly methods for counting time. Phases of the moon and the cycles of the sun provided a first method of observing the cycles of nature. Grains needed to be planted and harvested at the right time. Travelers, especially on the sea, needed reliable ways of determining their routes. Timing was a sacred matter. Religious influence is seen in all calendars. The public ordering of time today is generally set by governments and by commercial interests. This shift of responsibility creates the need for festivals, feasts and quiet times under religious auspices in order to preserve the rights of individuals and communities in a global community.

It is a challenge to discover the sacred times and community celebrations of greatest importance in each religious tradition.. Having conversation with local people and checking out the local newspapers/TV is effective. The Internet offers many useful resources. National holidays depend on the country and region. Local sources are necessary for accurate and timely information.

Christianity: Sunday is the usual day for worship although occasional services are held throughout the week as well. Sacred dates are focused on events in the life of Jesus and the early church that inform the faith life of the believer. A yearly cycle of observance is used in many Christian traditions and involves coordinated Bible readings. Lunar and solar calendars are used to set dates used globally. The religion teaches that time is moving in a direction which will ultimately be made complete in God. Primary Holy Days are Easter, Christmas and Good Friday.

Islam: Mid day Friday prayer services are weekly. Sacred dates are remembrance of events in the history of Islam. The entire world wide Muslim community has a cycle of life centered on these sacred observances. The dates are based on a lunar calendar and advance approximately 11 days each year. Daily prayers facing Mecca are practiced by Muslims.. Islam teaches that time is moving in a direction in keeping with Allah's intentions for humanity. Primary Holy times are Eid al Adha, Ramadan, and Eid al Fitr. Holy days begin the evening before the stated date. Moon sighting affects the exact day of observance and may vary from place to place.

Hindu: Hindu religious culture blends sacred with secular. The endless circle of existence means that festivals and special observances provide marking points in life. Ritual practices connect the present with past and future. Domestic and public rituals assist persons in moving the through various passages of life and assist in preparing for what is next. Movement is toward no further rebirths and becoming one with the ultimate reality – the universal Brahman or "world soul". Primary holy times are: Vaisakhi, Janmashtami and Diwali.

Buddhist: Life as a stream of becomings finds persons dealing with suffering in order to become enlightened and awakened. Reincarnation moves the person toward nirvana and freedom from suffering. Time, like all of life, is transient and not permanent. Time is the occasion of suffering and death as well as the setting for awakening from ignorance and finding Enlightenment. Meditation frees the mind from time and its distractions. Primary holy times are: Birthday of Buddha, Vesak and Magha Puja.

Chinese Religions - **Confucian/Daoist/Buddhist**: Time is the ebb and flow of the patterns of nature. Since life is focused on order and harmony the role of humanity is to keep the yin and yang of life in balance. Wisdom and the practical life of a nation are what govern the use of time for people. Rapid economic development in China today challenges Confucian humanism and order. Industrial time contrasts with the harmony of nature and human order. A primary holy day is the Chinese New Year.

Sikh: Time is the setting for human development that moves through birth and rebirth. Daily prayers are part of the disciplined movement toward human equality. The goal in life is to achieve liberation in release from the cycle of birth and death and become one with God. All of life and time is to be used to this end. Devotion to spiritual disciplines and Sikh principles is the calling of each Sikh. Primary holy times are: Baisaki, Diwali, and the Birthday of Guru Nanak.

Jewish: Sabbath, commemorating God's time of rest after the creation of the world, begins at sundown on Friday to sundown on Saturday. This primary sacred time is accompanied by an annual cycle of holy days commemorating historic happenings that are basic to the identity of the Jewish community. Time is understood as movement toward the reign of God in the whole creation. Primary holy times are: Rosh Hashanah, Yom Kippur and Pesach (Passover). Holy days begin at sundown the night before the stated date.

Baha'i: The vision of a united peaceful world energizes believers to gather often for prayers and teaching to keep the vision clear. In the future there may be other successor religions beyond Baha'i to carry on the human progression toward a unified planet. Primary holy days are Ridvan, Ascension of Baha'u'llha, and Naw Ruz. Holy Days begin the evening before the stated date.

Shinto: The use of time is focused on the attainment of the bright and pure mind. Ritual practices and shrines aid various rites of passage in the lives of individuals and communities. The rhythms and forms of nature lend an almost timeless atmosphere to the movement between the sacred and secular elements of daily life. Shrines offer festivals to mark seasonal changes with purification rites. Primary holy times are Shogatsu Matsuri, Tenjin Matsuri, and Spring Festival.

Jain: All life is focused on reaching higher levels of spiritual development. Festivals are connected with five major events in the life of the believer – entering the womb, birth, renunciation, attainment of omniscience and then final emancipation (death). The sense of time revolves around the processes of the ascetic life and offerings of gifts and service to the poor. Primary holy times are Paryushana and Diwali.

Wicca – Neo Pagan: The natural world rhythms of seasonal change are focal points for rituals and observations. Personal life is intertwined with natural observations. The solstices and equinoxes set the primary sacred times.

Indigenous Religions: Time is often a mythical concept accessed by stories, sacred places, and ecstatic rituals. Oral traditions pass on information about the ancient ones and great events that define the life of a community. Much of this information is private and not for public attention or curiosity.

Materialist – Atheist – Secular: Time is either a matter of scientific investigation, business efficiency, or commercial calendaring for most of these traditions. Contemplating a direction for time is a distraction from the business at hand. Time simply is. An immense calendar of business dates, personal observances, remembrance of national battles, victories, calamities and discoveries provide for holidays that mark national and commercial life.

A Quick Resource for at Home and Away

Cultural and Religious Taboos

The subjects of taboos is the final section in comparisons because it is the most mysterious and hidden realm of religious life. Rising out of the past experience of a people are certain feelings about places, foods, bodily functions, ways of speaking, and religious rituals. These realities are usually not consciously recognized by religious adherents or by visitors. Taboos are important for the visitor in particular so that respect can be shown and offense avoided.

This issue takes on importance when, in a global society, people of one culture are traveling to new situations constantly. Not wishing to offend ones host is critical to a pleasant and informative situation. Equally important are the positive approaches one can master. Particular sects or individuals may hold to rigid expectations.

The writing that follows barely touches the surface of this subject. The reader and traveler enter a classroom of learning that is mystery filled when dealing with cultural and religious taboos.

Christianity: Regulations regarding food and drink vary depending on the tradition and the country. Intemperate habits of any kind are usually seen as inappropriate. Manners of dress depend on the particular culture and congregation. Strong feelings about appropriate music and dress may be in effect from place to place. Alcohol usage is prohibited in some traditions and careless usage is always out of place.

Islam: No alcoholic beverages are permitted. Pork and lard are not to be touched or eaten. Public display of the body by women is not acceptable. Physical touch is off limits. Avoid public displays of affection. Be aware of the seriousness of offense in dominant Islamic regions. Avoid conversation about the nature of Allah or the Qur'an. In Arab culture the host sets topics of conversation. Do not greet with the left hand.

Hindu: In India vegetarian diets are common. The eating of beef or pork is particularly discouraged. The left hand is not to be used in eating or for greeting. A slight bow with palms of hands together is an appropriate greeting. Physical contact between men and women in public is to be avoided. An aggressive attitude is usually seen as a sign of disrespect.

Buddhist: Eating meat is not appropriate. Killing of creatures for food is frowned upon. Some Buddhists do use meat. Nonviolence is encouraged throughout society. Mahayana Buddhism includes schools of thought that discourage the use alcohol. The unique national and cultural expressions of Buddhism mean that the visitor must be open to learning local practices if taboo elements of society are to be understood. Respect is to be shown to leaders such as the Dalai Lama.

Chinese Religions - **Confucian/Daoist/Buddhist:** Avoid upsetting natural order and balance. The variety of Chinese customs and practices demands that the visitor be constantly learning from the unique environment being visited. All religions are wrapped into the Chinese way of life based on ancient history and front line modern thinking. Commerce holds a central place in Chinese life and affects religious expressions. The government keeps all religious expressions in view. Some religions are not permitted – all are part of the Chinese order and culture

Judaism: No use of pork or related products is allowed. Certain other foods are also prohibited. No work rules are binding for observant Jews beyond the observance of the Sabbath. Regulations regarding the preparation of food are of critical importance for many Jewish communities. If one is visiting a synagogue or temple guidance will be offered regarding dress, where to be seated, and how to act. The closeness of Jewish communities means that visitors are to understand themselves as guests at certain occasions.

Baha'i: Avoid alcohol and narcotics. Respect for the ideas and practices of Baha'i is expected. A positive response to the welcome offered to visitors is appreciated. As a world wide religion, local Baha'i communities will generally express local taboos but within in the bounds of Baha' teaching.

Sikh: The use of alcohol is discouraged. Respect for the dress, particularly of Sikh men, is expected. Wearing a turban and carrying a small knife or simulated knife are characteristic of members the Kahlsa, a brotherhood with firm standards for moral life and business practices.

Shinto: Japanese national cultural ways are infused throughout Shinto life. Lucky and unlucky numbers are one expression. The arrangement of flowers needs to be careful so as to not offend. Conversation ought not deal with certain subjects such as the Imperial system and the underclass. The proper use of chopsticks is important. Approaching and entering a temple is to be done in a respectful manner.

Jain: Avoid killing any creatures. Avoid showy life style and possessions. Show respect to monks. General taboos of the culture within which Jain people are located will likely be expressed. Once again, the visitor has an obligation to show respect, avoid treating Jain people like tourist objects, and learn how to see the religion as another way of expressing the sacred.

Wicca – Neo Pagan: Showing respect to manners of dress, speech and ritual is expected. Rituals may be quite private for individuals and groups. It is not appropriate to treat events as entertainment or a curiosity.

Indigenous: Individual and group practices are unique to each situation. The variety means that a visitor must be attentive and should not expect to understand what is happening or how actions or gestures will be interpreted. The sacred is located almost everywhere for the indigenous religious communities. They decide what is sacred and what this means. To take pictures or wander about without guidance can be very offensive. Showing respect is an elemental virtue for the visitor.

Non religious – Atheist – Secular: Religious conversation and practices are often inappropriate and offensive. Respect for centers of commerce, entertainment, and education is expected. There are ritual ceremonies, events and actions that are not to be disrespected. Sporting events carry many understandings not first apparent to the visitor. Check things out first rather than later.

Glossary

Glossary

Definitions that apply to words as used in this book.

Adherents – Persons who support a religion or cause.

Ahimsa – Belief in sacredness of all living beings. Buddhist and Hindu.

Allah – Islamic word for the Divine One.

Alms-giving – Giving money or goods for the poor.

Ascetic Life – A life of self denial and renunciation of material comforts.

Atheist – One who denies the existence of god or gods.

Bodhi Tree – Fig tree where Buddha attained enlightenment.

Bodhisattva – An enlightened one who forgoes nirvana to serve others. Buddhist and Hindu

Brahman – The supreme existence and fount of all things.

Buddha nature – The way of impermanence taught by Buddha.

Church – The community of Christians at one place or worldwide.

Common Era – A period coinciding with the Christian era.

Compassion – Awareness of the suffering of others.

Contemplation – Observation of and meditation on spiritual matters.

Covenant – God's binding agreement with the human race. Christian.

Culture – Collective attitudes and practices of an era or region.

Enlightenment – Buddhist or Hindu state of mind beyond desire.

Equinox – Sun crossing the celestial equator twice a year.

Eternal – Seemingly endless with no beginning or ending.

Festival – An occasion for feasting and/or celebration.

Gender – Sexual identity.

God – One that is worshipped or followed – may be supernatural or mythical.

Goddess – Female being with supernatural powers and attributes.

Gudwara – Sikh house of worship.

Guru Granth Sahib – The book compiled by Gurus

Hadith – The tradition or collection of traditions attributed to the Prophet Muhammad

Hajj – Pilgrimage to Mecca by Muslims.

Halal – Meat slaughtered in keeping with Islamic Sharia.

Haram – Actions not lawful for Muslims.

Hebrew Scriptures – The first 39 books of the Bible.

Hieroglyphics – A system of writing using pictorial symbols.

Humanism – A belief system centered on humans and rejecting religion.

Immortality – Endless life or existence.

Incarnation – Christian concept of the bodily appearance of Creator God as part of the Trinity of Creator, Savior and Spirit.

Indigenous – Occurring naturally in an area or environment.

Interfaith – A method for relating world religions that depends on conversation and eventual dealing with differences.

Islamization – Process of conforming cultures to Islamic laws and precepts.

Jihad – Muslim struggle against infidels and also personal striving for spiritual perfection.

Kalsa – Sikh fellowship of baptized persons who adhere to the principles taught by the Ten Sikh Masters.

Kami – Sacred being worshipped in Shinto – spirits in natural world.

Karma – Hindu and Buddhist idea of destiny or fate determined by the total actions and conduct of a person.

Koan – Zen Buddhist paradoxical statement or story used for awakening.

Kosher – Conforming to Jewish dietary laws and ritual purity.

Lunar calendar – Moon based system for organizing time.

Magic (Magick) – Causing change to occur by act of the will.

Martyrdom – Suffering and/or death for a belief or cause.

Meditation – Self-directed calming of the body and mind, often for religious purposes.

Mosque – Muslim house of worship and often a community center.

Mythical – Stories used by a culture or religion to present complex traditions.

Nirvana   A state of mind with great inner peace and contentment is the way to Buddhist happiness attained through enlightenment. Hindu emancipation from ignorance and attachment to the material world.

Oral Tradition – The spoken preservation of culture and ancestry.

Paradise – Abode of righteous souls after death. Christian.

Patriarchy – A social system governed by males.

Philosophy – Pursuit of wisdom by the intellect and logical reasoning.

Pilgrimage – Journey to a sacred place or shrine.

Relic – An object from ancient times that has sacred meaning.

Religion – Any belief system that gives ultimate meaning to life and that gathers adherents over time.

Renunciation – Giving up of something important to the self.

Sabbath – Seventh day of the week for Jews; First day of the week for Christians.

Sacred Text – Documents related to the worship of a deity or whatever may be declared as holy.

Scrolls – Document in the form of a roll of parchment or paper.

Sect – A group forming a distinct unit within a larger body.

Secular – Confined to human life on earth and excluding religion.

Shrine – A place of devotion or commemoration.

Solar Calendar – A calendar based on the tropical year– 365.24220 days.

Solstice – Two times of the year when the sun is at its greatest distance from the equator.

Standing Stones – Prehistoric monuments made of tall, upright stones.

Stupa – A Buddhist monument for Buddha or a saint which may commemorate an event or house a relic.

Synagogue – A Jewish building for worship and religious education.

Taboos – Bans based on social custom

Temple – A building dedicated to religious ceremonies.

The Tao – Taoist basic principle of the universe that transcends reality. The Confucian system of right manners of human conduct.

Theology – Study of the nature of God and of religious ideas.

Time – The continuum in which events occur from past to the present and on to the future. There are many other definitions.

Torri gate - Shinto understands this distinctive gate to be a transition point between the sacred shrine and the normal world.

Trajectory – A path followed by an organization or person.

Translation – The transferring of the meaning of a text or word from one particular language to another language

Transliteration – Transcribing the words of one language into the alphabet characters of another language.

Tribal – The culture and ways of groups made up of social units of ethnic or familial descent.

Trinity – Christian concept of the one God understood as creator, savior and living presence now

Ummah – The Muslim community or people.

Worship – Reverent love and devotion to a deity or sacred object.

Yin and Yang – In Chinese philosophy the two fundamental contrasting principles that interact with and balance people and nature.

Definition Resources include:

Answers.com

http://www.answers.com

TheFreeDictionary.com

http://www.thefreedictionary.com

Wikipedia.com

http://www.wikipedia.org/

Merriam Webster Online Dictionary

http://www.n-w.com/

Dictionary.laborlawtalk.com

http://dictionary.laborlawtalk.com/

Google.com

http://www.google.com

Primary Sacred

Observances

Primary Sacred Observances

Part 1: Regular Worship Practices

Christianity – Sunday is most widely observed day for worship in the community of believers. Some Christians observe the Sabbath on Saturday. Adherents are encouraged to practice frequent daily prayer and meditation.

Islam – Friday at midday is the time for Muslim men to gather for prayers – women share separately in prayers. All are expected to pray five times a day. All prayers can be said at one time in unusual circumstances.

Hindu – Various days of the week find people coming to the temple for prayer, petition and celebration. Shrines house figures of various deities and are tended by priests. Visitors come to show honor and offer prayers.

Buddhist – Shrines involving statues and paintings are in homes and temples and are places for showing devotion and to practice meditation and where teaching happens. No particular day of the week is dominant for worship.

Sikh – The Gudwara is a house of worship where services of devotion take place. There is no special day of worship. Worshippers honor Guru Granth Sahib at the Gudwara.

Judaism – The Sabbath is Friday sundown until Saturday evening and is the time for public gatherings for worship at the Synagogue. Assembly is for prayers, teaching and for the community to gather for holy days.

Baha'i – Daily worship by individuals using certain obligatory prayers is coupled with gatherings in private homes. The first day of each month is celebrated as a feast day.

Shinto – Shrines are important for places of gathering as rituals led by priests are observed. Home altars are used by some adherents. Daily observations are encouraged.

Chinese Religions – Festivals are the primary times of observation. Other practices depend on the tradition and the region.

Jain – Cycles of festivals and pilgrimages are linked to historic events. Personal observation of Jain life style is accompanied by honoring of important figures in the early morning every day.

Wicca – Neo Pagan – Natural earth cycles such as equinox and solstice form the basis for gatherings and for personal observations.

Part 2: Special Holy Days and Festivals

Christianity

Easter – This observance commemorates the new life of Jesus Christ after his death by crucifixion. This is the most important holy time for Christians.

Christmas – Celebration of the birth of Jesus Christ.

Good Friday – A solemn day of remembrance of the death, by crucifixion, of Jesus Christ.

Islam

Eid al Adha – This three day observance recalls the willingness of Abraham to submit to the will of Allah. This is the most important holy day for Muslims. It concludes the Hajj.

Eid al Fitr – This is a festival of thanksgiving to Allah for the values of the month of Ramadan.

Ramadan – The 9th month of the Islamic calendar is devoted to recalling Mohammad's reception of the divine revelation recorded in the Qur'an.

Hindu

Navaratri – Dussehra – Celebration of Durga, destroyer of evil.

Janmashtami – The birth of Krishna, an incarnation of Vishnu, is celebrated. Krishna's life is described in detail in celebrations involving sacred waters and prayers.

Diwali - Deepavali –This is the Festival of Lights that celebrates the victory of good over evil.

Buddhist

Vesak – The birth, enlightenment and death (attaining Nirvana) of Buddha are observed. It is the holiest of Buddhist sacred times.

Magha Puja – A celebration of the teaching of Lord Buddha, and affirmation of the Buddhist community, practices and traditions.

Dharma Day – The observation of the start of Buddha's teaching after his enlightenment. The Buddhist religion begins.

Sikh

Guru Nanak Birthday – The birth of the founder is celebrated

Baisaki – The beginning of the Khalsa brotherhood is observed.

Diwali – The Festival of Lights involving assemblies at Sikh temples.

Judaism

Yom Kippur - This Day of Atonement is the holiest day of the Jewish year. Jews ask forgiveness from G-d and people.

Rosh Hashanah – This day marks the beginning of a ten day period of penitence and spiritual renewal.

Pesach (Passover) – The deliverance of Israel from slavery is observed over a seven day period.

Baha'i

Ascension of Baha'u'llah – A day of remembrance for the founder who fearlessly proclaimed the message of God.

Naw-Ruz – The Baha'i New Year observance.

Declaration of the Bab – The anniversary of a message of universal peace to come with Baha'u'llah.

Shinto

Gantan-sai – New Years celebration. Also called Oshogatsu. Attention given to sincerity, constancy and renewed life.

Setsubun Sei – Equinox Day when ancestors are remembered. The end of winter is marked by casting out of evil.

Haru Matsuri – A springtime festival when girls are celebrated and a Peach Blossom Festival is recognized.

Chinese Religions

Chinese New Year – Observed by Buddhists, Taoist, Confucian and other religions of China.

Jain

Paryushana – Time of reflection, fasting and repentance that lasts from eight to ten days.

Diwali – Festival of Lights also observed by Hindus and Sikhs.

Mahavira Jayanti – Celebration of the birth of Lord Mahavira, the founder of modern Jainism.

Wicca – Neo Pagan

Samhain – A time of reflection at summer's end when the old is let go and the new is anticipated.

Beltane – The first day of summer when fertility is celebrated.

Solstice and Equinox observances – The change of seasons are observed.

The dates for holy days and definition of terms is available on-line at **http://www.interfaithcalendar.org**

Conversation with adherents of world religions in particular communities is necessary to discover local customs and observances.

Bibliography

Books and Web Sites

Bibliography
Books

Axtell, Roger: *Do's and Taboos Around the World.* New York
    John Wiley & Sons 1993

Bellenir, Karen: *Religious Holidays and Calendars: An
    Encyclopedic Handbook 3rd Edition.* Detroit, MI:
    Omnigraphics

Breuilly, Elizabeth, etc: *Religions of the World: The Illustrated
    Guide to Origins, Beliefs, Traditions & Festivals.* New
    York, N.Y.: Facts On File, Inc 1997

Doniger, Wendy: *Merriam-Webster's Encyclopedia of World
    Religions.* Springfield, MA: 1999

Edwards, Linda: *A Brief Guide to Beliefs: Ideas, Theologies,
    Mysteries and Movements.* Louisville: Westminster John
    Knox Press, 2001

Johnson, Sara Iles. *Religions of the Ancient World: A Guide.*
    Cambridge: MA Harvard University Press 2004

Levison, David: *Religion: A Cross Cultural Dictionary.* New
    York: Oxford University Press, 1996

Meredith, Susan: *The Usborne Book of World Religions.* London:
    Usborne Publishing Ltd, 1995

Smith, Huston: *The World's Religions.* San Francisco: Harper
    Collins, 1991

Web Sites

Christianity

Wikipedia http://en.wikipedia.org/wiki/Christianity

Catholic New Advent site -
http://www.newadvent.org/cathen/03712a.htm

Islam

Wikipedia   http://en.wikipedia.org/wiki/Islam

Islam.com http://www.islam.com/

Hindu

Wikipedia http://en.wikipedia.org/wiki/Hindu

The Hindu Universe http://www.hindunet.org/scriptures/

Chinese Traditional

Confucian

Wikipedia http://en.wikipedia.org/wiki/Confucianism

Religious Tolerance article
http://www.religioustolerance.org/confuciu.htm

Taoist

Wikipedia http://en.wikipedia.org/wiki/Taoist

Taoism Information Page
http://www.religiousworlds.com/taoism/index.html

Buddhist

Wikipedia http://en.wikipedia.org/wiki/Buddhism

Essentials of Buddhism http://www.buddhaweb.org/

Sikh

Wikipedia   http://en.wikipedia.org/wiki/Sikhism

All About Sikhs http://www.allaboutsikhs.com/home.php

Judaism

Wikipedia   http://en.wikipedia.org/wiki/Judaism

Judaism Introduction
http://library.thinkquest.org/28505/judaism/intro.htm

Baha'i

Wikipedia
http://en.wikipedia.org/wiki/Bah%C3%A1'%C3%AD_Faith

The Baha'is   http://www.bahai.org/

Shinto

Wikipedia   http://en.wikipedia.org/wiki/Shinto

Shinto Online Network
http://www.jinja.or.jp/english/s-0.html

Jain

Wikipedia   http://en.wikipedia.org/wiki/Jainism

Jainworld   http://www.jainworld.com/

Wicca-Neo Pagan

Covenant of the Goddess http://www.cog.org/

Pagan Federation http://www.us.paganfederation.org

Indigenous Religions

US Army Chaplains Library
   http://www.usachcs.army.mil/Library2/IndigReligMain.htm

African expressions
   http://members.aol.com/porchfour/religion/african.htm

Zoroastrian

Wikipedia http://en.wikipedia.org/wiki/Zoroastrianism

Zoroastrian archives http://www.avesta.org/

Zarathustrian Assembly - http://www.zoroastrian.org/

Materialist – Atheist – Secular

Secular Web Modern Library -
http://www.infidels.org/library/modern/nontheism/atheism/

American Atheists - http://www.atheists.org/

Nonreligious Worldview -
http://www.teachingaboutreligion.org/WorldviewDiversity/nonreli
gious_worldview.htm

Unitarian-Universalist
Wikipedia http://en.wikipedia.org/wiki/Unitarian_Universalism

Unitarian Universalist Association - http://uua.org/

Cao Dai
Wikipedia http://en.wikipedia.org/wiki/Cao_Dai

Home page http://www.caodai.org/pages/?pageID=1

Tenriko
Basic information http://www.tenrikyo.or.jp/

Juche
Wikipedia http://en.wikipedia.org/wiki/Juche

Study of the Juche Idea - http://www.cnet-ta.ne.jp/juche/defaulte.htm

Scientology
Wikipedia http://en.wikipedia.org/wiki/Scientology

Welcome to Scientology - http://www.scientology.org/

Rastafaria
Wikipedia http://en.wikipedia.org/wiki/Rastafarian

Religions in general

US Army Chaplains Center Library -
http://www.usachcs.army.mil/library2/Nav/main1.html

BBC – Religions and Ethics Religions

http://www.bbc.co.uk/religion/religions

Wikipedia on religious groups -
http://en.wikipedia.org/wiki/Major_religious_groups

Places of Peace and Power – www.sacredsites.com/

Sacred Sites International - http://www.sacred-sites.org/

Religions in the USA -
http://www.undergodprocon.org/pop/religionchart.htm

Project at U of Wyoming – has interesting glossary of terms

http://uwacadweb.uwyo.edu/religionet/er/default.htm

Interfaith Organization Web Sites

Council for a Parliament of the World's Religions
http://www.cpwr.org/

Greater Boston Interfaith Organization   www.gbio.org

Inter Faith Network for the United Kingdom
http://www.interfaith.org.uk/

Interfaith Alliance   http://www.tialliance.org/

Mall Area Religious Council http://www.meaningstore.com

North American Interfaith Network http://www.nain.org/

Religious Tolerance http://www.religioustolerance.org

The Interfaith Alliance UK   http://www.interfaithalliance.org.uk/

The Pluralism Project at Harvard University
http://www.fas.harvard.edu/

United Religions Initiative   http://www.uri.org/

World Interfaith Congress   http://www.interfaithcongress.org/

Web Sites describing food practices of various religions

General Foods and Religions sources:

Food Culture and Religion by the Better Food Channel of the
Victorian (Australia) Government
http://www.betterhealth.vic.gov.au/bhcv2/bhcarticles.nsf/pages/Fo
od_culture_and_religion?OpenDocument

Ceremonies related to foods -
http://www.nagpuronline.com/people/rit_mslm.html
Religion and Dietary Practices - http://www.faqs.org/nutrition/Pre-
Sma/Religion-and-Dietary-Practices.html

Vegetarian information - http://www.vegblog.org/resources/

Christians and Food

Christian Chefs Fellowship -
http://www.christianchefs.org/recipes.html

123Christians Christian Recipes –
http://www.123christians.com/christians/recipes/index.html

Muslims and Food

About Food - http://www.aboutfood.co.uk/spotlight/halal.html
Halal Foods - http://www.afic.com.au/Halal.htm

Hindus and Food

Hinduwebsite -
http://hinduwebsite.com/hinduism/h_food.asp

Hindu Dietary Practices -
http://hinduwebsite.com/hinduism/h_food.asp

Buddhists and Food

Answers.com on Buddhist Cusine -
http://www.answers.com/topic/buddhist-cuisine

Buddhist Faith Kitchen -
http://www.buddhistgateway.com/sites/kitchen/

Jewish Foods

Jewish Food Recipe Archives -
http://www.chebucto.ns.ca/~ab522/jewishfood.html

Jewish Recipes -
http://www.torahbytes.org/sechel/Jewish%20Recipes.htm

Chinese Foods – Confucian/Taoist/Buddhist

The Recipe Link - http://www.recipelink.com/rcpchinese.html
About: Chinese Cuisine - http://chinesefood.about.com/

Web Sites on Sacred Places

Places of Peace and Power –
http://www.sacredsites.com/index.html

Sacred Sites International – http://www.sacred-sites.org/

Sacred Destinations Travel Guide – http://www.sacred-destinations.com

Sacred Site Tours – http://www.saredsitetours.com

Web Sites on Map information

Maps of world religions – historical and contemporary

> http://www.wadsworth.com/religion_d/special_features/popups/maps/index.html

Maps and full listing of world countries and their primary religions.

> http://www.mapsofworld.com/world-religion-map.htm

Concentration of religions across the world

> http://www.godweb.org/religionsofworld.htm

Wikipedia article showing number and concentration

> http://en.wikipedia.org/wiki/Major_world_religions

About.com info on world's most popular religions

> http://geography.about.com/od/culturalgeography/a/popularreligion.htm

World outline map

> http://serc.carleton.edu/images/usingdata/nasaimages/world
> -map-outline.gif

Web Sites on News of Religion – These sites are

chosen because they appear to be relatively unbiased regarding any particular religion.

BBC Headline Religion News

> http://www.bbc.co.uk/religion/news/index.shtml

Netscape Religion Stories

> http://religion.netscape.com/

Religion and Ethics Newsweekly

> http://www.pbs.org/wnet/religionandethics/index.html

Religion News Service

> http://www.religionnews.com/index.html

Religion Review

> http://www.wnreligion.com/

World Wide Religion News

> http://www.wwrn.org/index.php

Yahoo Religion News

> http://news.yahoo.com/fc/world/religion

Interfaith Postscript

The word **"interfaith"** conjures up a host of different impressions and understandings. It is a concept that is evolving as the world becomes more interconnected and as people travel as never before.

Organizations focused on various aspects of Interfaith are springing up in many countries. The World Bank has a section entitled "Development Dialogue on Values and Ethics. Their web site http://web.worldbank.org has a page entitled "Interfaith Organizations" listing a variety of organizations, many with a global perspective.

Each Interfaith organization has a different function. Some, such as The Greater Boston Interfaith Organization, have a local approach. www.gbio.org/ Others, like The Council for a Parliament on the World's Religions, have a global perspective ranging over many years of experience. www.cpwr.org

Experience teaches that there are levels of Interfaith life that are each unique and appropriate at the right time and place.

- Recognition that other religions exist is an elementary level for the interfaith experience. Although this may seem self-evident the fact is that broad based religious information is quite limited throughout much of the world. Each religion is protective of its territory and may tend to blind adherents to other traditions.

- Knowledge about those other religions comes into play whenever a person awakes to the existence of the other

137

faith systems. First impressions make a critical impact on the viewer. The information lodged in a person's mind may well be broadened but the emotion and images first mentally recorded will persist, especially if they are frightening or negative. Pleasant impressions are a platform for particularly effective continued learning.

- Learnings of new knowledge about religions take place whenever personal contact happens as well in the context of exposure to documents, events, and places. It is at this stage that the interfaith process takes root. Elemental data about the historical roots of a religion take their place with the ideas held most dear by a tradition. Out of the sea of possible impressions a picture begins to take form and familiarity opens the mind to ideas that were overwhelmed by the very newness of the other religion.

- When taking courage to venture into the presence of another religion one may often be surprised at the sensation of looking in a new way upon ones own religious tradition. In dealing with ideas and experiences that are new, a person finds that self-examination is a part of the transaction. A new clarity about a person's religious ideas may occur. A new depth of belief and confidence in the tradition may fill a person with thanksgiving and passion.

- It is possible that disappointment with a familiar tradition may result from the excitement and charm of the new. This may be seen as either positive or negative. Others may well not understand why a person moves to another tradition and trouble in families and communities result.

- Conversation between persons of various traditions can result in greater understanding, rejection of the whole process, or angry exchanges of words and body language. This is especially true when contacts move beyond doing projects together or having initial informational conversations.

- Early conversations tend to focus on that which the involved parties have in common. At some point focus on the differences come to the foreground and dialogue becomes difficult and painful. The true creativity of the Interfaith process arises when persons persist in exploring the elemental differences between traditions. Nice words are replaced by the passions of dealing with reality in all of its harshness and grandeur. Participants recognize that they will likely never be in agreement and yet they both respect and honor the other person's convictions. Learning with body as well as mind can take place in such encounters.

Here is a possible scenario illustrating the Interfaith Principle.

- People of good will of various religions begin group conversations to get to know each other as individuals.

- They move on to conversations about what they may do together to live out the principles that they have found workable in their life together to this point.

- Projects arise that can be done. Organization takes place so that things can be done in an orderly manner. Time is taken by increasing ventures details.

- The satisfaction of doing things together opens the way for conversations that begin to deal with some elemental beliefs of the involved traditions. The mix of personalities begins to become more visible as people become themselves in the interfaith happening.

- Working and talking becomes more demanding as emotions rise to the surface and normal human protective reactions happen. Individuals begin to wonder where this is going and what is happening to the pleasant environment of early times.

- A sense of hopeful anxiety arises from the gathered people as they recognize the hard demands of the interfaith process. At this point the adventure depends on the gathered leadership of all the involved people. No guidelines will guarantee that the venture will move to a next best step. Interfaith is a continuing experiment in human religious discovery.

Here is the down-to-earth basis for the ideas stated above.

- In 1987 several Christian pastors in the neighborhood of the soon to be Mall of America in Bloomington, Minnesota, USA, began to have discussions on what a large commercial development would mean to near by religious organizations and to the community in general.

- By 1990 an interfaith organization, The Mall Area Religious Council (MARC), was formed involving Christian, Jewish, Muslim, Baha'i, Hindu and Unitarian Universalist participants. For complete information regarding MARC and its history go to http://www.meaningstore.org

- In preparation for spiritual presence at Mall of America, the MARC members came to know one another's faith perspective on a personal working basis.

- An annual holiday display brought this variety of people together to face the public in the person of shoppers. On occasion Southern Baptist Christian and Buddhist would

  find themselves together presenting the MARC case for religious understanding. In any event, people became personally acquainted across religious lines.

- In 2000 an interfaith store, The Oasis, was opened and for six months presented interfaith presence to the shopping public. Work on development and management of the store brought this variety of people into intimate working contact as they related with fellow store workers and the public.

- By 2006 the organization was involving 40 congregations of representing most of the major world religion traditions. Strains begin to show as persons come to know each other better and feel more at ease in expressing deeply held feelings and religious convictions. Changes of leadership have put new people into responsibility and the history of the organization has moved beyond its formative stages.

- All financial support has come from participating congregations and individual persons. No foundation money or large corporate grants have been received. A harsh financial discipline has helped maintain the work and participation ethic of MARC.

- In 2006 the Mall Area Religious Council involved the following religious and community groups of the Minnesota metropolitan area: Cedar Valley Church (Assemblies of God); Local Spiritual Assemblies of Baha'is in Bloomington; Southtown Church in Bloomington (Baptist); Word of Grace Baptist; Monastery and Meditation Center of Tibetan Buddhism; St. Bonaventure Catholic Community; Church of the Assumption (Catholic); Christian Church (Non-denominational); Christian Science Reading Room; Saints Mary and Martha Church (Episcopal); Mandir Hindu Temple; Masjid An Nur Islamic Center; Jewish Community Relations Council of Minnesota and the Dakotas; Christ the King Church (ELCA Lutheran); Easter Church (ELCA Lutheran); Grace by the Mall Lutheran (ELCA); Holy Emmanuel Lutheran Church (LCMS); House of Prayer Church (ELCA Lutheran); Woodlake Church Lutheran (ELCA Lutheran); St. Elizabeth Orthodox Mission; Parliament of World's Religions; Potter's House of Jesus Christ (Pentecostal); Peace Church (Reformed Church in America); Riverside Church (Reformed Church in America); Oak Grove Presbyterian; Edgecumbe Presbyterian; Minnesota Valley Fellowship (Unitarian Universalist); Emerson Congregational Church of Christ (United Church of Christ); Advent Church (United Methodist); Church of Peace (United Methodist); Hillcrest Church (United Methodist); Normandale Hylands Church (United Methodist); Portland Avenue Church (United Methodist); River Hills Church (United Methodist); Unity South; Fort Snelling Memorial Chapel; Workplace Ministries; Southdale Y's Mens Club; Club Recovery Inc.

Out of this twenty year crucible of experience there has been a wealth of interfaith learning. As a participant leader in MARC for most of its history, I bring to this book the conviction that contact between world religion participants makes a difference for the good of the local community and the global scene.

Delton Krueger

AFTERWORD

Surfing the Tide of World Religions

A rising tide of interest in World Religions accompanies the growing presence of religion. The situation presents a challenge in knowing how to take hold of such a vast and detailed ocean of information and experience. This may be when choice of a right metaphor can be of assistance.

We conclude this book with the metaphor of Surfing. This activity happens at the edge of the sea and can be both fun and dangerous. It takes practice to avoid getting dumped into the sand head first. Gaining skill provides the heady experience of unpredictability, body contact, speed and the safety of shore near at hand.

There is widespread evidence that the tide of religions is rising all across the globe. When all things are changing rapidly people look for the dependable and the traditional. The instantaneous electronic communication experience is shrinking the globe so that religions once isolated and local now become a public curiosity as well as faith system.

World Religions are this vast sea of people, unique events and customs, endless variety of ideas and doctrines, as well as traditions, sacred sites and holy days. One can get lost in this intricate complexity and be deeply touched by the appeal of one religion or the other.

This is an invitation to apply the learnings of Sea Surfing to the process of exploring the edges of the ocean of religion. World Religion Surfing. This book is a trip to the edge of the stormy Religion Sea and a look at the immense tide that is rising.

Let's go! The Surf is up!

Index

A Quick Resource for at Home and Away

Indigenous

Islam

Jain

A Quick Resource for at Home and Away

About the Author

Delton Krueger is a writer and developer of religions information.

In "Portable Guide to World Religions" the author responds to the desire for accessible basic information about the religions of the 21st century world.

Experience in the field of religion includes interfaith experience at the Mall of America in Minnesota; work with congregations and regional religious bodies; and participation in interfaith ventures for over five decades. He is a Christian with ordination in the United Methodist Church of the Wesleyan tradition. Advanced religious education was at Drew University Theological School at Madison, New Jersey, USA. Undergraduate work was at Hamline University in St. Paul, Minnesota, USA.

The Internet aspect of World Religions information has, since 1995, been addressed by www.interfaithcalendar.org – a web presentation of the primary sacred times of the world religions, including a ten year projection of calendar dates.

The site was developed by Delton Krueger at the beginning of the public presence of the Internet. Interfaithcalendar.org is now used in over 140 countries. Curious individuals, students, planners in governmental, educational, business, and religious organizations make use of this resource.

A Quick Resource for at Home and Away